Encounters with God

The Book of ACTS

Encounters with God Study Guide Series

The Gospel of Matthew
The Gospel of Mark
The Gospel of Luke
The Gospel of John
The Acts of the Apostles
The Book of Romans

Encounters with God

The Book of ACTS

Copyright © 2007 by

Henry Blackaby, Th.M., D.D.
Richard Blackaby, M.Div., Ph.D.
Thomas Blackaby, M.Div., D.Min.
Melvin Blackaby, M.Div., Ph.D.
Norman Blackaby, M.Div., B.L., Ph.D.

Published by Thomas Nelson, Inc., P.O. Box 141000, Nashville, Tennessee 37214.

Scripture quotations are taken from The New King James Version® (NKJV), copyright 1979, 1980, 1982, 1992 Thomas Nelson, Inc., Publishers.

Library of Congress Cataloging-in-Publication Data
ISBN 1-4185-26428

Printed in the United States of America

07 08 09 10 RRD 9 8 7 6 5 4 3 2 1

CONTENTS

Encounters with God

The Book of ACTS

AN INTRODUCTION TO THE ACTS OF THE APOSTLES

The book of Acts is the fifth book of the New Testament and the sequel to the Gospel of Luke—it is a bridge between the Gospel accounts of Jesus' life and ministry and the epistles, letters written to the early church. It is a book about the beginning of the church and its empowerment by the Holy Spirit for divine action in the whole world, not only the Jewish world, but the Gentile world; in other words, how the gospel spread from a small group of disciples into a worldwide phenomenon.

Acts has been titled in various Bible translations as "Acts" or "Acts of the Apostles." The book makes very little mention of the apostles other than Peter and Paul. John is mentioned only three times, and then, as a companion of Peter. Early church members Stephen and Philip are given more verses than the apostles. Much of the book presents the conversion and ministry of Paul, who took on the title of apostle but was not a follower of Jesus during Jesus' lifetime.

Like the Gospel of Luke, the book of Acts is addressed to Theophilus, who may have been a Roman official but was clearly a Gentile. The name in the Greek language literally means *lover of God* and this book may have been written for all Gentile believers or to a particular community of believers. Luke and Acts were originally circulated as one complete and independent history.

The prologue of the Gospel of Luke states the author's desire to give an *orderly account* of the origins of Christianity (Luke 1:1–4). Acts continues that account. As a Gentile, Luke exemplifies the Hellenistic style of recording history. The book does not simply keep records or chronicle events, but it encourages the reader and offers an apologetic for the Christian church. It tells how the Holy Spirit orchestrated the expansion of the gospel, and used individuals for His divine purposes in the decades immediately following Christ Jesus' death, resurrection, and ascension.

The author of Acts addresses several specific concerns. First, Christians were being charged with sedition and Acts was written, in part, to defend Christianity as a legitimate movement. It argues Christianity was the continuation of the Jewish faith and the proper fulfillment of Israel's religion. Second, the disciples of Jesus were mandated to make disciples of all nations (Luke 24:46–49). Acts relates how the gospel moved from Jerusalem to Rome in less than thirty-five years. Third, the power behind the gospel's expansion is clearly identified as the Holy Spirit. Christianity has spread, Luke contends, by the power of the Spirit, not as the result of human reasoning, planning, or popularity. The Holy Spirit is central to the book of Acts and is mentioned more than fifty times. The Spirit is presented as being promised by Jesus (Acts 1:4), guiding the disciples in many ways, and the One actively compelling Jesus' ongoing ministry through His followers. The work of the Holy Spirit is presented as orderly, miraculous, joyful, and effective—within individuals, in the church, and ultimately in the world.

The book of Acts has been considered a major source of inspiration through the centuries to those who are looking for evidence that God is active in the world. It answers questions Christians continue to ask today:

- How can a small group of believers engage in effective evangelism?

- How can a person make a difference in today's world?

- What is central to a presentation of the gospel?

- How does the world respond to gospel?

Luke the Author. Luke is generally accepted as the author of Acts. He was a physician Paul met in Troas (Acts 16:8–11) and from that point on in Luke's narrative of Acts, a number of sections include the personal pronoun *we*, indicating that Luke was a participant and eyewitness to the events. Luke was called the *beloved physician* in Paul's writing (see Colossians 4:14) and apparently was both Paul's traveling companion in ministry as well as his attending physician (Colossians 4:14; 2 Timothy 4:11; and Philemon 24). The book ends with Paul's imprisonment in Rome. Historians date that imprisonment at 60 AD, and since Acts makes no mention of Jerusalem's collapse in 70 AD, or Nero's persecution of Christians after Rome's fire in 64 AD, most believe the book was written between 62 and 65 AD.

AN OVERVIEW OF OUR STUDY OF THE BOOK OF ACTS

This study guide presents seven lessons drawn from and based largely on the book of Acts. The study guide elaborates on, and is based on, the commentary included in the *Blackaby Study Bible*:

Lesson #1: Empowered to Witness

Lesson #2: Empowered to Serve

Lesson #3: Empowered to Heal

Lesson #4: Empowered to Deliver from Evil

Lesson #5: Empowered to Hurdle Man-Made Barriers

Lesson #6: Empowered to Overcome Death

Lesson #7: Empowered to Endure and Persevere

Personal or Group Use. These lessons are offered for personal study and reflection, or for small-group Bible study. The questions may be answered by an individual reader, or used as a foundation for group discussion. A segment titled "Notes to Leaders of Small Groups" is included at the back of this book to help those who might lead a group study of the material.

Before you embark on this study, we encourage you to read in full in the *Blackaby Study Bible* titled "How to Study the Bible" on pages viii–ix. Our contention is always that the Bible is unique among all literature. It is God's definitive word for humanity. The Bible is

- *inspired*—God breathed

- *authoritative*—absolutely the final word on any spiritual matter

- *the plumb line of truth*—the standard against which all human activity and reasoning must be evaluated

The Bible is fascinating in that it has remarkable diversity, but also remarkable unity. The books were penned by a diverse assortment of authors representing a variety of languages and cultures. The Bible as a whole has a number of literary forms. But, the Bible's message from cover to cover is clear, consistent, and unified.

More than mere words on a page, the Bible is an encounter with God Himself. No book is more critical to your life. The very essence of the Bible is the Lord Himself.

God speaks by the Holy Spirit through the Bible. He also communicates during your time of prayer, in your life circumstances, and through the church. Read your Bible in an attitude of prayer, and allow the Holy Spirit to make you aware of God's activity in and through your personal life. Write down what you learn, meditate on it, and adjust your thoughts, attitudes, and behavior accordingly. Look for ways every day in which the truth of God's Word can be applied to your circumstances and relationships. God is not random, but orderly and intentional in the way He speaks to you.

Be encouraged—the Bible is *not* too difficult for the average person to understand if that person asks the Holy Spirit for help. (Furthermore, not even the most brilliant person can fully understand the Bible apart from the Holy Spirit's help!) God desires for you to know Him and His Word. Every person who reads the Bible can learn from it. The person who will receive maximum benefit from reading and studying the Bible, however, is the person who:

- *is born again* (John 3:3, 5). Those who are born again and have received the gift of God's Spirit have a distinct advantage in understanding the deeper truths of His Word.

- *has a heart that desires to learn God's truth.* Your attitude greatly influences the outcome of Bible study. Resist the temptation to focus on what others have said about the Bible. Allow the Holy Spirit to guide you as you study God's Word for yourself.

- *has a heart that seeks to obey God.* The Holy Spirit loves to teach those who have a desire to apply what they learn. Begin your Bible study with prayer, asking the Holy Spirit to guide your thoughts and to impress upon you what is on God's heart. Then, make plans to adjust your life immediately to obey the Lord fully. As you read and study the Bible, your purpose is not to *create* meaning, but to *discover* the meaning of the text with the Holy Spirit's guidance. Ask yourself, "What did the author have in mind? How was this applied by those who first heard these words?" Especially in your study of the Gospel accounts, pay attention to the words of Jesus that begin "Most assuredly" or "He opened His mouth and taught them, saying." These are core principles and teachings that powerfully impact every person's life.

At times you may find it helpful to consult other passages of the Bible (made available in the center columns in the *Blackaby Study Bible*), or the commentary that is in the margins of the *Blackaby Study Bible*.

Keep in mind that Bible study is not primarily an exercise for acquiring information, but an opportunity for transformation. Bible study is your opportunity to encounter God and to be changed in His presence. When God speaks to your heart, nothing remains the same. Jesus said, "He who has ears to hear, let him hear" (Matthew 13:9). Choose to have ears that desire to hear!

The B-A-S-I-Cs of Each Study in This Guide. Each lesson in this study guide has five segments, using the word BASIC as an acronym. The word BASIC does not allude to elementary or simple, but rather to *foundational*. These studies extend the concepts that are part of the *Blackaby Study Bible* commentary and are focused on key aspects of what it means to be a Christ-follower in today's world. The BASIC acronym stands for:

B = *Bible Focus*. This segment presents the central passage for the lesson and a general explanation that covers the central theme or concern.

A = *Application for Today*. This segment has a story or illustration related to modern-day times, with questions that link the Bible text to today's issues, problems, and concerns.

S = *Supplementary Scriptures to Consider*. In this segment, other Bible verses related to the general theme of the lesson are explored.

I = *Introspection and Implications*. In this segment, questions are asked that lead to deeper reflection about one's personal faith journey and life experiences.

C = *Communicating the Good News*. This segment presents challenging questions aimed at ways in which the truth of the lesson might be lived out and shared with others (either to win the lost or build up the church).

LESSON #1

EMPOWERED TO WITNESS

Witness: someone who heard or saw something that happened and gives evidence about it

B
Bible Focus

> *And being assembled together with them, He commanded*
> *them not to depart from Jerusalem, but to wait for the*
> *Promise of the Father, "which," He said, "you have heard*
> *from Me; for John truly baptized with water, but you shall be*
> *baptized with the Holy Spirit not many days from now."*
> *Therefore, when they had come together, they asked Him,*
> *saying, "Lord, will You at this time restore the kingdom to*
> *Israel?" And He said to them, "It is not for you to know*
> *times or seasons which the Father has put in His own author-*
> *ity. But you shall receive power when the Holy Spirit has*
> *come upon you; and you shall be witnesses to Me in*
> *Jerusalem, and in all Judea and Samaria, and to the end of*
> *the earth" (Acts 1:4–8).*
>
> *When the Day of Pentecost had fully come, they were all*
> *with one accord in one place. And suddenly there came a*
> *sound from heaven, as of a rushing mighty wind, and it filled*
> *the whole house where they were sitting. Then there appeared*
> *to them divided tongues, as of fire, and one sat upon each of*
> *them. And they were all filled with the Holy Spirit and began*
> *to speak with other tongues, as the Spirit gave them utter-*
> *ance.*
>
> *And there were dwelling in Jerusalem Jews, devout men,*
> *from every nation under heaven. And when this sound oc-*
> *curred, the multitude came together, and were confused,*
> *because everyone heard them speak in his own language.*
>
> *Peter, standing up with the eleven, raised his voice and*
> *said to them, "Men of Judea and all who dwell in Jerusalem,*
> *let this be known to you, and heed my words" (Acts*
> *2:1–6,14).*

The earliest Christians understood baptism in light of their traditional Jewish customs of purification. Jews routinely entered into pools of water until they were fully immersed, as a sign of their renewed commitment to obeying and trusting God and His Word as a righteous Jew. They believed they emerged from this ritual cleansed before God and thus, acceptable for making temple sacrifices or engaging in synagogue service. Those John the Baptist baptized entered into the Jordan River until fully immersed as a sign of repentance and return to God. The early Christians who were baptized also entered waters until fully immersed, but this time with a commitment to obeying and trusting in the name of Jesus. They believed they were cleansed from sin and made acceptable for Christ-honoring service and sacrifice. Even today, Christians are baptized in water for these purposes.

Jesus said the baptism of the Holy Spirit would have a slightly different character. This baptism was for those who were already believers in Christ Jesus. It was a baptism in which the person would be totally engulfed and indwelled by the Holy Spirit. That Spirit would come with "fire" to purify and cleanse each person to be a holy vessel for Him to use. Only then could a believer keep Jesus' commands and be available to tell others about Him. The sure sign a person was filled with the Holy Spirit was a love for Christ and a compelling drive to follow Him as He took them into the world as a witness to the gospel.

In telling His disciples about the Holy Spirit, Jesus made it very clear that the kingdom of God would be established and directed by the Spirit. The disciples originally had a very narrow view of the Kingdom as a political renewal and restoration of Israel's kingdom. Jesus, however, redirected their concern *outward*—away from their immediate spheres of influence to other nations and the global purposes of God.

Immediately after the disciples experienced the rushing baptism of the Holy Spirit, people who were in Jerusalem for Celebration of Pentecost gathered to hear Peter speak to them, and each person heard the gospel in his own language. What a miracle! It was a miracle that immediately launched the message and power of the gospel far beyond Jerusalem. Literally thousands were baptized that day in the name of Jesus, and the church was birthed out of the heart of God. Most of those who had come from other nations who heard the gospel and were baptized that day returned to their homelands. Their stories are not told in the book of Acts, but no doubt are recorded in heaven. The apostles didn't initiate or orchestrate anything about this miraculous day—their part was simply to release their lives to the Holy Spirit and allow Him to do the Lord's work through them.

This is the same challenge we each face today as Christians.

Are we willing to enter *fully* into the baptism of Jesus Christ—more than just our physical bodies immersed in water, but our entire lives immersed, cleansed, and filled by the Holy Spirit? Are we willing to sacrifice our time, energies, and talents to His purposes, fully submitting our lives to Him?

Are we willing to receive the Holy Spirit into our lives? Are we willing to lay aside our own human-based agendas and goals and go where the Holy Spirit leads us to go, say what He directs us to say, and do what He compels us to do?

The Holy Spirit does not act apart from our will, but neither does He allow us to act in sovereign and supernatural ways apart from His will.

A
Application for Today

"Watcha doin', Grandpa?" the little boy asked.

"Cleaning up this old lamp," Grandpa said as he polished the antique vessel in his hands.

"What for?" the boy asked.

"So I can fill it with this pure oil," Grandpa replied as he looked at the lamp closely, and then reached for a jug of oil nearby.

"What for?" the boy continued to ask.

"So I can put this wick in it and light it," said Grandpa, inserting a wick and then lighting it.

"What for?" the boy asked.

Grandpa carried the lighted lamp to a table nearby and then leaned over to look directly into the eyes of his young grandson and said: "You'll know the reason when it gets dark."

You are God's vessel in this world (2 Corinthians 4:7).

The oil of the Holy Spirit indwells you (Psalm 23:5; John 14:16–17).

Your purpose is to be Christ's light in a darkened world (Matthew 5:14–16).

Being a good, cleaned-up lamp isn't enough. Having oil in your lamp isn't enough. It takes being a lamp filled with oil and set afire with purpose, passion, and a proclamation of the gospel to change the world for Christ!

To what extent are you allowing your heavenly Father to prepare you for His service?

S
Supplementary Scriptures to Consider

After a lame man had been healed at the Beautiful Gate, Peter and John preached in the portico of the temple, where they were arrested by the religious authorities. Peter and John then spoke boldly before the Sanhedrin, the high priest, and other priests. Unable to charge them with any crime, the apostles were released, but with an admonition they neither speak nor teach in the name of Jesus. They refused those terms. The religious leaders again threatened them and let them go. Peter and John then returned to their companions and reported all that had happened. Rather than advise caution, they prayed for *boldness* in continuing to speak and teach!

> "For truly against Your holy Servant Jesus, whom You
> anointed, both Herod and Pontius Pilate, with the Gentiles and
> the people of Israel, were gathered together to do whatever

Your hand and Your purpose determined before to be done.
Now Lord, look on their threats, and grant to Your servants
that with all boldness they may speak Your word, by stretching
out Your hand to heal, and that signs and wonders may be
done through the name of Your holy Servant Jesus."

And when they had prayed, the place where they were
assembled together was shaken; and they were all filled with
the Holy Spirit, and they spoke the word of God with boldness" (Acts 4:27–31).

• Have you ever experienced a time in which you prayed for boldness?
  What happened? (Recall a specific situation.)

• Have you ever spoken with greater boldness and found that God took you
  into situations you never thought possible? What happened? (Recall a
  specific situation.)

• Notice that Peter and John said Herod, Pontius Pilate, the Gentiles, and the people of Israel were *"gathered together to do whatever Your hand and Your purpose determined before to be done"* (Acts 4:27–28). How do you respond to their conclusion?

What is a person's perspective if he believes all things happen according to God's purposes? Does such a perspective add to boldness in witnessing?

Stephen, one of the chosen deacons in the early church, gave this witness to the religious leaders of Jerusalem:

> And Stephen, full of faith and power, did great wonders and signs among the people. Then there arose some from what is called the Synagogue of the Freemen (Cyrenians, Alexandrians, and those from Cilicia and Asia), disputing with Stephen. And they were not able to resist the wisdom and the Spirit by which he spoke. Then they secretly induced men to say, "We have heard him speak blasphemous words against Moses and God." And they stirred up the people, the elders, and the scribes; and they came upon him, seized him, and brought him to the council.

> Then the high priest said, "Are these things so?"
> And he said, "Brethren and fathers, listen . . ."

When they heard these things they were cut to the heart, and they gnashed at him with their teeth. But he, being full of the Holy Spirit, gazed into heaven and saw the glory of God, and Jesus standing at the right hand of God, and said, "Look! I see the heavens opened and the Son of Man standing at the right hand of God!"

Then they cried out with a loud voice, stopped their ears, and ran at him with one accord; and they cast him out of the city and stoned him. . . . And they stoned Stephen as he was calling on God and saying, "Lord Jesus, receive my spirit." Then he knelt down and cried out with a loud voice, "Lord, do not charge them with this sin." And when he had said this, he fell asleep (Acts 6:8–12; 7:1–2,54–60).

- Stephen, the first martyr, is described as a man *"full of faith and power"* who *"did great wonders and signs among the people"* (Acts 6:8). As a Christian filled with the Holy Spirit, do you aspire to this description? Why or why not?

- What would you say if someone accused you of blasphemy when you gave witness to Christ Jesus?

- Notice those who heard Stephen initially were *"not able to resist the wisdom and the Spirit by which he spoke"* (Acts 6:10).

Have you ever found yourself irresistibly drawn to a message marked by *"wisdom and the Spirit"* (Acts 6:10)? How did this impact your own desire to know the Lord? How did it impact your desire to give voice to your witness about Jesus Christ?

The Holy Spirit directly led Philip to give witness to a foreign dignitary:

> Now an angel of the Lord spoke to Philip, saying, "Arise and go toward the south along the road which goes down from Jerusalem to Gaza." This is desert. So he arose and went. And behold, a man of Ethiopia, a eunuch of great authority under Candace the queen of the Ethiopians, who had charge of all her treasury, and had come to Jerusalem to worship, was returning. And sitting in his chariot, he was reading Isaiah the prophet. Then the Spirit said to Philip, "Go near and overtake this chariot."
> So Philip ran to him, and heard him reading the prophet Isaiah, and said, "Do you understand what you are reading?" (Acts 8:26–30).

• Have you ever experienced the Holy Spirit telling you to speak to a specific person you might otherwise never have approached? What happened? (Recall a specific incident.)

• If you perceived someone as having great authority, what might keep you from approaching them with the gospel? How might you overcome your hesitancy?

Several times in the book of Acts, the apostle Paul gave witness to those who had authority over his life. He said this to King Agrippa:

> "Therefore, King Agrippa, I was not disobedient to the heavenly vision, but declared first to those in Damascus and in Jerusalem, and throughout all the region of Judea, and then to the Gentiles, that they should repent, turn to God, and do works befitting repentance. For these reasons the Jews seized me in the temple and tried to kill me. Therefore, having obtained help from God, to this day I stand, witnessing both to small and great, saying no other things than those which the prophets and Moses said would come—that the Christ would suffer, that He would be the first to rise from the dead, and would proclaim light to the Jewish people and to the Gentiles" (Acts 26:19–23).

• What does Paul's phrase *not disobedient to the heavenly vision"* (Acts 26:19) mean to you? Paul freely shared what we would call his personal testimony. Have you ever given your personal testimony to someone? What did you say? Many people find it helpful to write down their personal testimony. Consider doing this.

• Paul emphasized repentance and doing works *befitting repentance* (Acts 26:20). How do you define *repentance*? What do you consider to be works befitting repentance in your own life?

• Paul witnessed *to small and great* (Acts 26:22). Do you find it easier to share the gospel with certain groups of people more than others? Why do you believe this is so?

I
Introspection and Implications

1. Has the Holy Spirit empowered you to be Christ's witness? What does it mean to be indwelled by God's own Spirit?

2. Did you notice an increased boldness and desire to share the gospel with other people after you yielded your life to the Holy Spirit?

3. What are the main stumbling blocks you have experienced to your sharing the gospel? How did you overcome them, or how *might* you overcome them?

4. In what ways do you rely daily on the Holy Spirit for direction and guidance for your life?

5. How would you discern the Holy Spirit was prompting you to give witness to Christ Jesus? (Think of a specific situation or relationship.)

C
Communicating the Good News

Note again Paul said to King Agrippa that he preached about Christ's painful death and resurrection as the focal point for his witness. In what ways is it important to retain this focus as we give witness to Christ Jesus? How does your personal testimony reflect Christ's death and resurrection?

When was the last time you brought up the name of Jesus in a conversation with an unbeliever? What happened?

LESSON #2

EMPOWERED TO SERVE

*Service: work done by a person for
the benefit of someone else—generally as
a job, duty, punishment, or favor*

B
Bible Focus

> *So continuing daily with one accord in the temple, and breaking bread from house to house, they ate their food with gladness and simplicity of heart, praising God and having favor with all the people. And the Lord added to the church daily those who were being saved (Acts 2:46–47).*

> *Now the multitude of those who believed were of one heart and one soul; neither did anyone say that any of the things he possessed was his own, but they had all things in common. And with great power the apostles gave witness to the resurrection of the Lord Jesus. And great grace was upon them. Nor was there anyone among them who lacked; for all who were possessors of lands or houses sold them, and brought the proceeds of the things that were sold, and laid them at the apostles' feet; and they distributed to each as anyone has need. And Joses, who was also named Barnabas by the apostles (which is translated Son of Encouragement), a Levite of the country of Cyprus, having land, sold it, and brought the money and laid it at the apostles' feet (Acts 4:32–37).*

Jesus did four main things on the last night He was with His disciples. Each of these things has direct bearing on the way the first Christians treated one another. The first church in Jerusalem reflected each of them.

First, Jesus had supper with His closest disciples. During that supper, He took bread, gave thanks and broke it, and gave it to His disciples, saying, "This is My body which is given for you; do this in remembrance of Me." Then He took a cup after supper and said, "This cup is the new covenant in My blood, which is shed for you. This do, as often as you drink it, in remembrance of Me." (See Luke 22:19–20 and 1 Corinthians 11:23–26.)

Bread was the first item served in any Middle Eastern meal, primarily because it was used to sop up or scoop up food from other communal dishes placed on a table. Wine or juice was the last course, considered something of a dessert for its sweetness and also as an aid to digestion. A meal was considered complete if it only had bread and beverage, but most major meals also had vegetables; condiments of various types including nuts, dates, raisins, and yogurt; fruit; and on special occasions, meat. Jesus was presenting Himself as the beginning and ending of a "full meal." He was encouraging His disciples to partake of His life as the staple of all they needed (bread) and the joy of their souls (wine). To be sure, He had given them His life. Daily, Jesus had devoted His time and energy completely to teach, preach, and heal. He was about to pour out His blood on their behalf on the cross. Jesus was urging them to remember always how He had lived, what He had taught and done during His life, and why He had died. He admonished His disciples, in essence, to "remember Him" every time they sat down to have fellowship together.

Second, Jesus washed their feet. Doing the work of a servant, Jesus said to them, "You call Me Teacher and Lord, and you say well, for so I am. If I, then, your Lord and Teacher, have washed your feet, you also ought to wash one another's feet. For I have given you an example, that you should do as I have done to you. Most assuredly, I say to you, a servant is not greater than his master; nor is he who is sent greater than he who sent him. If you know these things, blessed are you if you do them" (John 13:13–17).

Third, Jesus taught the disciples a number of key lessons, all in the context of love. He admonished them to keep His commandments, to remember His love, and to love one another. Jesus promised them the Holy Spirit as the emissary and seal of God's love, and encouraged them to rely on the Holy Spirit to lead them, counsel them, and give them peace even in times of persecution. (See John 14—16.)

Fourth, Jesus prayed for His followers to be steadfast in their faith as they declared God's truth and love by both word and deed. (See John 17.)

In turn, Jesus' disciples did what He had modeled for them.

The early church was marked by the believers sharing meals, serving and caring for one another in very practical ways, recalling and studying the commands and teachings of Jesus, and remaining prayerful and steadfast *daily* in their new lives of faith, truth, and love.

The church grew *daily* as a result. People saw how the Christ-followers loved and cared for one another, and they heard the apostles' beliefs as it was taught in the temple each day. As a result, they wanted to be in fellowship with them.

To be a Christ-follower was to face intense persecution in the months that followed Christ's crucifixion, resurrection, and ascension. The Jewish religious authorities who had hated Jesus also hated those in the early church. They insisted those who professed Jesus as the Christ be put out of the synagogues. Many of the new believers lost their businesses or jobs, and some lost their families and homes. Part of what it meant for the early Christians to love one another involved sacrificing materially to help those believers who had material and financial needs.

There is no mention in the book of Acts about fund drives—there are no sermons about the importance of caring for the poor. The early church simply loved as Jesus had loved, sacrificially and generously. The power of the Holy Spirit in their midst compelled them to do so.

How do you describe the ministry and overall nature of your church today?

Are members in *fellowship* with one another—having meals together and encouraging one another as they *remember Christ* in all they do together?

Are members *serving* one another—caring for both practical and spiritual needs?

Are members *loving* one another—are leaders teaching the Word with power and are the parishioners reminding and encouraging one another to obey the commandments of God, all with a loving attitude?

Are members *praying for* one another that all might be faithful and steadfast in their witness of Christ Jesus?

If not, why not? What can be done?

A
Application for Today

Many churches have membership drives from time to time. Some call these revivals or neighborhood outreaches. Some churches often hold special events during Christmas and Easter holidays—so members might invite their unchurched or unsaved friends and neighbors to an event at the church that will be inspirational, joyful, Christ-centered, and generally "non-threatening." The goal is to bring people to the church building and into the context of the church community so the Holy Spirit might woo them to Christ.

How does our approach today differ from that of the first believers in Jerusalem?

How important is it we remain in close fellowship with other Christians, sharing our lives with them daily?

How important is it we do our utmost to make sure our fellow believers have their material, financial, and practical needs met?

A popular chorus among many Christians during the last thirty years has this as its refrain: "And they'll know we are Christians by our love, by our love—yes, they'll know we are Christians by our love."

How potent is a reputation for being loving?

S
Supplementary Scriptures to Consider

Matthias was chosen to replace Judas and to serve the church in the capacity of an apostle:

> Of these men who have accompanied us all the time that
> the Lord Jesus went in and out among us, beginning from the

baptism of John to that day when He was taken up from us, one of these must become a witness with us of His resurrection."

And they proposed two: Joseph called Barsabas, who was surnamed Justus, and Matthias. And they prayed and said, "You, O Lord, who know the hearts of all, show which of these two You have chosen to take part in this ministry and apostleship from which Judas by transgression fell, that he might go to his own place. And they cast their lots, and the lot fell on Matthias. And he was numbered with the eleven apostles" (Acts 1:21–26).

• The job of the apostle at that time was to serve the newly formed church through prayer, studying the Word, and then preaching and teaching about Jesus. How important is it to know that a person who serves the church in this way has been *"with Jesus"* for a significant amount of time? How important is it to know God has chosen this person?

• Do we place the same priorities on our full-time ministers today (prayer, studying the Word, and preaching and teaching about Jesus)?

• How do you respond to the fact Matthias was chosen by the casting of lots? This method of discerning God's will included asking God to guide their process and existed prior to the giving of the Holy Spirit at Pentecost. In what ways do we discern today if a person is appropriate for full-time ministry?

The early church was marked by mutual service to another. As noted previously, many of the new Christians were persecuted for their faith in Jesus and lost their jobs or were rejected by their families. Caring for one another was very practical—including food and other daily necessities. Adequate and fair caring required a degree of administration:

> Now in those days, when the number of disciples was multiplying, there arose a complaint against the Hebrews by the Hellenists, because their widows were neglected in the daily distribution. Then the twelve summoned the multitude of the disciples and said, "It is not desirable that we should leave the word of God and serve tables. Therefore, brethren, seek out from among you seven men of good reputation, full of the Holy Spirit and wisdom, whom we may appoint over this business; but we will give ourselves continually to prayer and to the ministry of the word."
>
> And the saying pleased the whole multitude. And they chose Stephen, a man full of faith and the Holy Spirit, and Philip, Prochorus, Nicanor, Timon, Parmenas, and Nicolas, a proselyte from Antioch, whom they set before the apostles; and when they had prayed, they laid hands on them. Then the word of God spread, and the number of the disciples multiplied greatly in Jerusalem, and a great many of the priests were obedient to the faith (Acts 6:1–7).

- Identify several specific ways in which the service of godly administrators is important to the overall functioning of a church.

- In what ways is it important to have people of *good reputation, full of the Holy Spirit and wisdom* (Acts 6:3) appointed over the business of the church?

The early church experienced a tremendous example of how *not* to engage in service!

> But a certain man named Ananias, with Sapphira his wife, sold a possession. And he kept back part of the proceeds, his wife also being aware of it, and brought a certain part and laid it at the apostles' feet. But Peter said, "Ananias, why has Satan filled your heart to lie to the Holy Spirit and keep back part of the price of the land for yourself? While it remained, was it not your own? And after it was sold, was it not in your own control? Why have you conceived this thing in your heart? You have not lied to men but to God."
>
> Then Ananias, hearing these words, fell down and breathed

his last. So great fear came upon all those who heard these things. And the young men arose and wrapped him up, carried him out, and buried him.

Now it was about three hours later when his wife came in, not knowing what had happened. And Peter answered her, "Tell me whether you sold the land for so much?"

She said, "Yes, for so much."

Then Peter said to her, "How is it that you have agreed together to test the Spirit of the Lord? Look, the feet of those who have buried your husband are at the door, and they will carry you out." Then immediately she fell down at his feet and breathed her last. And the young men came in and found her dead, and carrying her out, buried her by her husband. So great fear came upon all the church and upon all who heard these things (Acts 5:1–11).

• What does it mean to lie to God? How critical is this matter, especially in light of Jesus' teaching that the devil is the father of all who lie (John 8:44)?

• How does deception impact the functioning of the church today? How does deception limit the way in which the Holy Spirit might use a person or group of people?

• Ananias and Sapphira did not *need* to give everything to the Lord's work, but they did need to be honest in what they gave. Their error was in saying they had given all, when in truth, they had only given part. They sought the favor of people rather than the favor of God. How can we guard against this same tendency in our service to others?

I
Introspection and Implications

1. Early church believers are described as having *gladness and simplicity of heart* (Acts 2:46). Are these words that describe you? If not, what brings about such an attitude and how can you obtain it?

2. The early church was noted for *praising God and having favor with all the people* (Acts 2:47). Does this describe your personal life? Does this describe your church? If not, what is it about your relationship to God that needs help?

3. The book of Acts says *the multitude of those who believed were of one heart and one soul* (Acts 4:32). Does this describe your church? If not, how might the Holy Spirit use your life to inspire such an atmosphere?

4. In what specific ways are you personally involved in caring for others in your church?

5. How do you define *Christian service*? Is everything a person does for others an act of service? In what ways is it important that the Holy Spirit direct our service to others?

6. Are we to serve nonbelievers in the same way we serve fellow believers? If there are differences, what are they?

C
Communicating the Good News

If you were to develop a caring team for your church, how would you define its purpose and describe its activities? Who would you want involved on such a committee?

Describe the profile of the ideal caregiver.

Lesson #3

EMPOWERED TO HEAL

*Lame: unable to move in the
way one desires*

B
Bible Focus

> *Now Peter and John went up together to the temple at the*
> *hour of prayer, the ninth hour. And a certain man lame from his*
> *mother's womb was carried, whom they laid daily at the gate of*
> *the temple which is called Beautiful, to ask alms from those who*
> *entered the temple; who, seeing Peter and John about to go into*
> *the temple, asked for alms. And fixing his eyes on him, with*
> *John, Peter said, "Look at us." So he gave them his attention,*
> *expecting to receive something from them. Then Peter said,*
> *"Silver and gold I do not have, but what I do have I give you:*
> *In the name of Jesus Christ of Nazareth, rise up and walk." And*
> *he took him by the right hand and lifted him up, and immedi-*
> *ately his feet and ankle bones received strength. So he, leaping*
> *up, stood and walked and entered the temple with them—*
> *walking, leaping, and praising God. And all the people saw him*
> *walking and praising God. Then they knew that it was he who*
> *sat begging alms at the Beautiful Gate of the temple; and they*
> *were filled with wonder and amazement at what had happened*
> *to him.*
>
> *Now as the lame man who was healed held on to Peter and*
> *John, all the people ran together to them in the porch which is*
> *called Solomon's, greatly amazed. So when Peter saw it he*
> *responded to the people: "Men of Israel, why do you marvel at*
> *this? Or why look so intently at us, as though by our own power*
> *or godliness we had made this man walk? The God of Abra-*
> *ham, Isaac, and Jacob, the God of our fathers, glorified His*
> *Servant Jesus, whom you delivered up and denied in the pres-*
> *ence of Pilate, when he was determined to let Him go. But you*
> *denied the Holy One and the Just, and asked for a murderer to*
> *be granted to you, and killed the Prince of life, whom God*
> *raised from the dead, of which we are witnesses. And His name,*
> *through faith in His name, has made this man strong, whom you*
> *see and know. Yes, the faith which comes through Him has given*
> *him this perfect soundness in the presence of you all" (Acts*
> *3:1–16).*

Three o'clock in the afternoon was a regularly scheduled prayer time in the temple. For the apostles Peter and John, the hour no doubt had special signifi-cance—Jesus had died precisely at three o'clock. Their thoughts were likely on Jesus and His sacrificial love as they came to the gate called Beautiful and encountered a crippled man. This man was sitting at the boundary between the Court of the Gentiles and the Court of the Women. Because he was lame, he wasn't allowed to go any further into the temple. He had never been in the Court of the Jews, which was beyond the Court of the Women—the court he no doubt had dreamed of entering his entire life. In our terms today we might say that he was an outsider.

Peter and John had seen Jesus heal a lame man on more than one occasion. They had seen Jesus fix His eyes on someone in a crowd and know in His Spirit that the time had come for that person with a longstanding ailment to be healed. They had seen Jesus heal a person who had been in a disabled condition from birth. (See John 9:1–3.) Perhaps most importantly, they had heard Jesus say to His disciples, "Most assuredly, I say to you, he who believes in Me, the works that I do he will do also; and greater works than these he will do, because I go to My Father. And whatever you ask in My name, that I will do, that the Father may be glorified in the Son. If you ask anything in My name, I will do it" (John 14:12–14).

Peter and John *believed* what Jesus had said! They did not act on a whim— they acted on their faith in Jesus as the Holy Spirit led them.

Notice four things Peter and John did. First, they focused their attention on this man and insisted he focus his attention on them. They made contact, deep eye-to-eye contact. Few people gave alms in such a manner. Generally passersby tossed coins in the direction of a beggar. Few beggars ever had eye-to-eye contact with someone as they begged. They called for alms as if calling to the wind. They received alms from people who remained anonymous to them.

Second, Peter and John gave what they had of greatest value. It wasn't money. Very often we lose sight of the fact that what we have of greatest value cannot be measured or calculated. Your God-imparted wisdom, knowledge, compassion, developed skills and talents, friendship, faith, and most of all, your relationship with Jesus Christ are far more valuable than anything material you possess. Peter and John called upon this man to expect something *beyond* the normal copper coins he had been receiving for years. They raised his level of hope.

Third, Peter commanded this man, in the name of Jesus, to rise up and walk. Peter didn't offer this as a suggestion for the man's consideration. He ordered him to act.

Fourth, Peter took this man by the right hand and lifted him up. It was *as he lifted him,* that the man received strength into his bones and was enabled to walk. This forty-year-old man, who had never walked, not only could walk, but he leaped about and praised God as he went with Peter and John through the Court of the Women into the Court of the Jews!

What would have happened if Peter and John had ignored this man?

What would have happened if Peter and John had failed to believe Jesus and take Him at His word? In the absence of faith, what is the best we can give people?

What would have happened if Peter and John had merely tossed a little money into the beggar's basket?

What would have happened if they had not connected with this man in the way they did, had not commanded him as Peter commanded him, or lifted him up as Peter did?

Do you long to experience more of God's miracle-working power in and through your life to others? What must be done?

A
Application for Today

The woman opened her door and was disappointed. The two people standing at her doorstep were not holding the bag of groceries she was expecting. Nor were they handing her an envelope with cash in it, which is what she really would have preferred. The woman had found a leaflet under her door asking if she needed help, and she had called the number on the bottom of the leaflet. She had been surprised to learn the leaflet was from a church—but she was desperate and figured she'd put up with a little God talk if necessary. She had been assured someone would come to her home later that day. The church members had come, alright, but without food or money.

"We'd like for you and your children to come with us," one of the people at the door said.

"Where to?" the woman asked.

"We want you to walk down to the grocery store with us," said the church representative.

The woman was wary but felt she had little choice but to go with them to a grocery store a block away.

For their part, the church members recognized quickly the woman had been drinking. They were relieved when the woman said her children were staying with her sister in a neighboring apartment building. They were glad for a sunny warm day, and knew the walk would do the woman good.

The church members took the woman to the grocery store and helped her choose nutritious foods, and then upon returning to her apartment, they helped her unload the sacks of groceries. "Would you let us cook a meal for you?" one of them asked. The woman agreed. By now she was starting to sober up. The church members prepared three large pots of food—soup, stew, spaghetti—and put most of the food into containers for the freezer. The project took two hours, and just as the pots were being cleaned up, the woman's two children arrived home with their aunt by their side. The aunt was impressed by what she saw *and* by what she tasted. The church members sat down with the four people in the family and shared the meal they had prepared.

During the meal, the church members told how the Lord had helped them personally. The woman and her sister were surprised to learn that the two people from the church had grown up in their very neighborhood, and that they had been on welfare only three years before.

"I didn't know how to get or keep a job," one of the church members said. "I didn't know how to shop for the right foods or cook them." The other church member chimed in, "I didn't even know what I didn't know!"

Then one of the church members offered, "We'd like to help you, if you'll let us. We'd like for you to live a better life than the one you've been living. We believe God can help you just like He helped us. Will you give us a chance to show you how much God loves you?"

All of this happened on a Monday. The church members met with the family daily for two to three hours an evening—helping the woman clean her apartment, sort through a sack of clothing they had brought from the church's clothes closet, and talking about the love of the Lord. Because the woman knew the church members were coming each evening, she stayed sober. On Saturday evening, the church members led this woman, her two children, and the aunt to the Lord. On Sunday, they all went to church together.

In what ways are people who are stuck in poverty—or stuck in a welfare system—*lame*? What kinds of *mobility* do they lack?

How were the two church members the *body of Christ* to this family, even before this woman, her sister, and children ever walked in the doors of a church?

Would you describe what happened in the lives of this woman, her sister, and the two children a healing miracle? Why or why not? What was the fullness of healing that likely occurred in the days and weeks ahead?

In what ways did this act of caring require courage on the part of the two church members?

In what ways did the two members of this church give what they had to give, which went far beyond what the woman had requested?

S
Supplementary Scriptures to Consider

Peter and the other apostles traveled a great deal in the early days of the church, preaching and healing:

> Then the churches throughout all Judea, Galilee, and Samaria had peace and were edified. And walking in the fear of the Lord and in the comfort of the Holy Spirit, they were multiplied.
>
> Now it came to pass, as Peter went through all parts of the country, that he also came down to the saints who dwelt in

Lydda. There he found a certain man named Aeneas, who had
been bedridden eight years and was paralyzed. And Peter said
to him, "Aeneas, Jesus the Christ heals you. Arise and make
your bed." Then he arose immediately. So all who dwelt at
Lydda and Sharon saw him and turned to the Lord (Acts
9:31–35).

• In what ways do healing miracles attract attention and cause people to be
more receptive to hearing the gospel?

• Note the phrase that all who dwelt at Lydda and Sharon saw him—the
man who had been healed—and turned to the Lord. The focus was on the
person healed, not on Peter. How important is it that we credit Christ
Jesus when we are healed?

• In what ways do healing miracles help increase faith among believers?

• If you had encountered Aeneas, what would you have said or done? Why or why not?

Paul was bold in his reaching out to a foreigner who had assisted him and others after a shipwreck:

> In that region there was an estate of the leading citizen of the island, whose name was Publius, who received us and enter- tained us courteously for three days. And it happened that the father of Publius lay sick of a fever and dysentery. Paul went in to him and prayed, and he laid his hands on him and healed him. So when this was done, the rest of those on the island who had diseases also came and were healed. They also honored us in many ways; and when we departed, they provided such things as were necessary (Acts 28:7–9).

• How did the Holy Spirit arrange circumstances so many people on the island might be healed? Have you ever felt the Holy Spirit set things in motion in some way to provide you with an opportunity to preach, teach, or give witness to Jesus?

- No mention is made in this incident of people accepting Christ Jesus as their Savior. How do you respond to the idea that people may have been healed but did not receive Jesus as Savior?

I
Introspection and Implications

1. Jesus said, "Most assuredly, I say to you, he who believes in Me, the works that I do he will do also; and greater works than these he will do" (John 14:12). What does this statement mean to you?

2. How do you define *healing*? What aspects of healing are always supernatural?

3. Does healing happen in stages? At various degrees?

4. Identify several things you have to give to others that are more valuable than money.

5. A man once said, "It is God's job to heal and save. It is my job to pray and tell." How do you respond to that statement? What stands in the way of our praying and telling? How might we overcome those obstacles?

6. Have you ever prayed for someone to be healed? What happened? How did you feel in the aftermath? How did the person for whom you prayed respond or feel?

C
Communicating the Good News

How important is it to make a real heart-to-heart, eye-to-eye connection with people to whom you are sharing the gospel or for whom you are praying? What keeps us from establishing such an intense connection? How might we overcome our resistance to communicating in this way?

LESSON #4

EMPOWERED TO DELIVER FROM EVIL

Magic: conjuring tricks and illusions that make apparently impossible things seem to happen
Sorcery: the use of magic
Divination: methods or practices related to foretelling the future through omens or oracles

B
Bible Focus

> Now God worked unusual miracles by the hands of Paul,
> so that even handkerchiefs or aprons were brought from his
> body to the sick, and the diseases left them and the evil spirits
> went out of them. Then some of the itinerant Jewish exorcists
> took it upon themselves to call the name of the Lord Jesus
> over those who had evil spirits, saying, "We exorcise you by
> the Jesus whom Paul preaches." Also there were seven sons of
> Sceva, a Jewish chief priest, who did so.
>
> And the evil spirit answered and said, "Jesus I know, and
> Paul I know; but who are you?"
>
> Then the man in whom the evil spirit was leaped on them,
> overpowered them, and prevailed against them, so that they
> fled out of that house naked and wounded. This became
> known both to all Jews and Greeks dwelling in Ephesus; and
> fear fell on them all, and the name of the Lord Jesus was
> magnified. And many who had believed came confessing and
> telling their deeds. Also, many of those who had practiced
> magic brought their books together and burned them in the
> sight of all. And they counted up the value of them, and it
> totaled fifty thousand pieces of silver. So the word of the Lord
> grew mightily and prevailed (Acts 19:11–20).

Occult practices were rampant in the ancient world. Men and women in all
nations, and especially it seems in ancient Middle Eastern cultures, were
eager to discover "hidden knowledge." This was done primarily by interpreting dreams or other signs, which were often peculiarities in the sacrifices
offered to an idol. Several major sorts of divination were practiced; among
them were: analyzing unusual phenomenon in water, fire, earth, or air;
watching the flight of birds and listening to their birdsongs; interpreting
dreams, looking at the entrails of sacrificed animals; and reading the tea
leaves or coffee grounds of emptied and overturned cups.

The point of all these practices was to gain knowledge of a person's
destiny and knowledge of what to do or expect in the future.

The Law of Moses stood in sharp opposition to such practices. Divination
was among those things that were called an *abomination* to the Lord. (See
Leviticus 19:31; 20:6 and Deuteronomy 18:9–13.) The teachings of Jesus and
the early church also stood against all forms of occult practice.

Was God opposed to people understanding their destiny or purpose in life?
Did God want to keep His people *in the dark* when it came to knowing what

to do or say or how best to prepare for the future? Did God want His people to refrain completely from understanding the *signs of the times* or the prevailing trends of the societies around them? Not at all!

What God commanded His people was trust Him and Him *alone* to give them meaning and purpose. He commanded them to rely on Him and to obey His commandments, and in doing both, to develop godly character. In turn, as a natural outflow of their character, their knowledge of God's Word, and their reliance on the Holy Spirit, they would know what to do in any situation. Jesus made it clear His followers were to understand the prevailing trends of society, which fluctuate and change, and to understand even more the prevailing truth of God for all men at all times, which does not fluctuate or change.

Rather than rely on an *omen*, God requires we rely only *on Him*.

Rather than read tea leaves, God requires we read the leaves of His Word.

Rather than turn to a palm reader, God requires we place ourselves in the palm of His hand.

Two things in the incident described in Acts 19 are worthy of special attention.

First, the Jewish exorcists were using the name of Jesus as an incantation (Acts 19:13). These exorcists had no faith in Jesus. They were not *in Christ*. The name of Jesus has power, but only to those who believe and who have taken on the identity of Christ Jesus as their own identity.

Second, the books that were burned in Ephesus were not only how-to books related to magic (Acts 19:19). The pagan temple in Ephesus was noted for the production of oracles—little scraps of paper wrapped up and placed in silver amulets worn around a person's neck. A person paid to have his future told by so-called diviners in the pagan temple there. They also purchased their silver amulets at the temple, paying fees according to the weight of the silver in the necklace. The oracle inside the amulet was commonly called the *book* of that person's life—it told their destiny. Those who turned to Christ took off their silver amulets, emptied them of the oracles, and burned the oracles. This was an outward and visible sign of their inward and invisible commitment—they now were trusting in God's Word rather than the word of pagan men. The silver amulets were given to the church treasury to be melted and sold. The value of these necklaces was tens of thousands of dollars in today's currency.

This incident concludes with the statement, *The word of the Lord grew mightily and prevailed* (Acts 19:20). Evil spirits overpowered and prevailed over the sons of Sceva who did not believe in Jesus. In direct contrast, the Word of God prevailed over the work of evil spirits in those who believed!

Where are people turning today for information about who they are and what purpose they might have? Where are people turning in their search for meaning in life?

Where are people turning for information about the future of our nation and our world?

How does evil overpower a person who pursues the occult?

In what ways are we wise to understand the trends of society? Why is it important to have this understanding? How can we keep from being discouraged by those trends? How might we go about changing ungodly trends?

Are we Christians truly willing to trust *only* in God to reveal to us what we need to know about ourselves, our personal future, and the future of the world?

A
Application for Today

Did you read your horoscope in the newspaper today? If so, you joined several million other people in the United States and Canada who do so on a regular basis. Horoscopes are widely available—in newspapers, magazines of many types, and Internet sites. Astrologers who offer personalized readings often charge great sums of money.

Do you read the statement tucked into the fortune cookie at the end of your meal at a favorite Oriental restaurant? It's hard not to!

Do you eagerly read or listen to the person who professes to know what is going to happen next, especially if that person is predicting the Second Coming of Christ or the end of the world?

Is it right to do so?

"But," you may be saying, "I only do these things for amusement, or to be 'informed' about what is being said or taught."

The truth is, we each absorb to some degree and at some level, every piece of information we take into our minds. We may not *think* some of the things we perceive, hear, read, or talk about lodges and takes root in us, but brain research studies have shown repeatedly that *all* perceptions are lodged in memory. The conscious mind may not access all perceptions, but all are registered subconsciously. It is out of both our conscious and subconscious minds that we form ideas, opinions, attitudes, and beliefs—and out of our ideas, opinions, attitudes, and beliefs, we speak and act.

Ask yourself, "Can I read the paper and *not* read my horoscope, or look at the horoscope page in the magazine and quickly turn past it?" "Can I eat the cookie and *never* open the fortune to read it?" "Can I turn off the person who claims with great authority to know precisely when future events will occur?" If your answer is "no" or "not very easily," what can you conclude about the potency of hidden knowledge?

S
Supplementary Scriptures to Consider

Paul encountered a sorcerer—a false prophet—on his first missionary journey:

> Now when they had gone through the island to Paphos, they found a certain sorcerer, a false prophet, a Jew whose name was Bar-Jesus, who was with the proconsul, Sergius Paulus, an intelligent man. This man called for Barnabas and Saul and sought to hear the word of God. But Elymas the sorcerer (for so his name is translated) withstood them, seeking to turn the proconsul away from the faith. Then Saul, who also is called Paul, filled with the Holy Spirit, looked intently at him and said, "O full of all deceit and all fraud, you son of the devil, you enemy of all righteousness, will you not cease perverting the straight ways of the Lord? And now, indeed, the hand of the Lord is upon you, and you shall be blind, not seeing the sun for a time." And immediately a dark mist fell on him, and he went around seeking someone to lead him by the hand. Then the proconsul believed, when he saw what had been done, being astonished at the teaching of the Lord (Acts 13:6–12).

• What are the hallmarks of this sorcerer's character according to Paul? In what ways are these the hallmarks of all who engage routinely in occult practices?

• Paul very likely saw himself in a battle for the soul of Sergius Paulus. In what ways are all of us in a battle when spiritual truth is presented to us?

Paul and Silas encountered a slave girl with a spirit of divination while they were in Philippi:

> Now it happened, as we went to prayer, that a certain slave girl possessed with a spirit of divination met us, who brought her masters much profit by fortune-telling. This girl followed Paul and us, and cried out, saying, "These men are the servants of the Most High God, who proclaim to us the way of salvation." And this she did for many days. But Paul, greatly annoyed, turned and said to the spirit, "I command you in the name of Jesus Christ to come out of her." And he came out that very hour (Acts 16:16–18).

• The spirit in this slave was factual in what it said. Paul and Silas *were* men who were servants of the Most High God, and they were proclaiming the way of salvation. What was wrong with this slave girl's outcries?

• How important is it that the life of a messenger and the truth of the message line up as being *right* before God?

• What happens when Christians are shown favor by evil people?

• What happens when public attention is diverted to the people who are preaching the gospel, and away from Jesus, who is the gospel?

In the Law of Moses, to practice divination, magic, and other occult activities was classified as *abomination* to the Lord:

> When you come into the land which the LORD your God is giving you, you shall not learn to follow the abominations of those nations. There shall not be found among you anyone who makes his son or his daughter pass through the fire, or

one who practices witchcraft, or a soothsayer, or one who interprets omens, or a sorcerer, or one who conjures spells, or a medium, or a spiritist, or one who calls up the dead. For all who do these things are an abomination to the LORD, and because of these abominations the LORD your God drives them out from before you. You shall be blameless before the LORD your God. For these nations which you will dispossess listened to soothsayers and diviners; but as for you, the LORD your God has not appointed such for you (Deuteronomy 18:9–15).

And . . .

Give no regard to mediums and familiar spirits; do not seek after them, to be defiled by them: I am the LORD your God.

And the person who turns to mediums and familiar spirits, to prostitute himself with them, I will set My face against that person and cut him off from his people (Leviticus 19:31 and 20:6).

- An *abomination* is something that evokes an extremely intense dislike or disapproval of something as being immoral, disgusting, or shameful. Is there ever such a thing as *acceptable* dabbling in the occult?

- What does it mean to be cut off from your people? How do occult practices separate a person from God's people today?

I
Introspection and Implications

1. How do you go about discerning the purpose for your life?

2. How do you feel about the future? Are you cautious, hopeful, fearful, hesitant, optimistic, faith-filled? On what do you base your feelings?

3. How do you discern the trends of the times? Do you ever adjust your witness of Christ Jesus to the trends you see around you?

4. How do you differentiate between genuine prophecy and occult divination?

5. Are you afraid of evil spirits? Why or why not? How does a person who fears evil spirits confront them? How can a person overcome fear of evil?

C
Communicating the Good News

In the book of Acts, evil spirits are depicted as standing in the way of a person coming to know Jesus Christ as Savior. Do evil spirits function in this way today? What can be done to free people from evil influences and help them accept Jesus Christ?

LESSON #5

EMPOWERED TO HURDLE MAN-MADE BARRIERS

*Barrier: anything that obstructs or separates,
often by emphasizing differences; something
considered to be a limitation or boundary*

B
Bible Focus

Peter went up on the housetop to pray, about the sixth hour. Then he became very hungry and wanted to eat; but while they made ready, he fell into a trance and saw heaven opened and an object like a great sheet bound at the four corners, descending to him and let down to the earth. In it were all kinds of four-footed animals of the earth, wild beasts, creeping things, and birds of the air. And a voice came to him, "Rise, Peter; kill and eat."

But Peter said, "Not so, Lord! For I have never eaten anything common or unclean."

And a voice spoke to him again the second time, "What God has cleansed you must not call common."

This was done three times. And the object was taken up into heaven again.

Now while Peter wondered within himself what this vision which he had seen meant, behold, the men who had been sent from Cornelius had made inquiry for Simon's house, and stood before the gate. And they called and asked whether Simon, whose surname was Peter, was lodging there.

While Peter thought about the vision, the Spirit said to him, "Behold, three men are seeking you. Arise therefore, go down and go with them, doubting nothing; for I have sent them."

Then Peter went down to the men who had been sent to him from Cornelius, and said, "Yes, I am he whom you seek. For what reason have you come?"

And they said, "Cornelius the centurion, a just man, one who fears God and has a good reputation among all the nation of the Jews, was divinely instructed by a holy angel to summon you to his house, and to hear words from you." Then he invited them in and lodged them.

On the next day Peter went away with them, and some brethren from Joppa accompanied him.

Then he [Peter] said them, "You know how unlawful it is for a Jewish man to keep company with or go to one of another nation. But God has shown me that I should not call any man common or unclean" (Acts 10:9–23,28).

One of the most ancient unwritten laws is the law of hospitality. It has been extremely important for thousands of years in the Middle East, where life has often depended on the hospitality extended by total strangers.

In ancient Bible times, a nomadic family—leading its flocks and herds from pastureland to pastureland, and from water well to water well—lived a fairly isolated life. According to the law of hospitality, strangers who arrived at the family's tent were to be given food and shelter. The underlying expectation was this: Should the nomadic family ever be in similar need, they could turn to others they met in the wilderness and be given nourishment and safe haven. Those with whom a person *broke bread* were considered part of the family for the length of their stay. The host family was under obligation to defend the visitor, even to the point of death, as long as the visitor was in the shelter of the family's tents.

The Law of Moses was very generous toward widows, orphans, and strangers. The strangers, however, were prohibited from participating in Jewish religious rituals and festivals, except the Feast of Tabernacles, and the Jews were not to marry people of other religions or races.

Whenever possible, Jews were required to refrain from mingling socially with Gentiles. They were considered *unclean*, and any Jew who came into close contact with a Gentile was required to undergo various purification rituals before he could participate fully in the life of the synagogue or make sacrifices in the temple.

In a vision, Peter saw a sheet lowered from heaven. It was filled with animals that were considered *unclean* or *common*—foods a Jew was commanded never to eat. Yet the voice from heaven told Peter to *Rise, kill, and eat* (Acts 10:13). This was done three times, a sure sign this repeated command was from God. Then God told Peter that *unclean* or *common* men were about to show up at his door, men He had sent.

It is difficult for us to comprehend fully how shocking this must have been to Peter, a Christian who was also a righteous Jew.

It happened just as God said. Peter's response was to *lodge them* (Acts 10:23). In that simple act of hospitality, the barrier between Jew and Gentile was broken when it came to sharing the gospel and extending Christian love!

Is there a person or a group of people with whom you cannot imagine ever having any kind of association—perhaps people of another race, religion, nationality, social class, or economic status? We like to think of ourselves as being nondiscriminatory and tolerant, but virtually all people have prejudice to some degree regarding a type of person they'd prefer to avoid. Their prejudice may not be open or harsh, but it exists nonetheless—perhaps only in a subtle feeling of discomfort when a certain type of person comes around.

What would you do if the Lord led you to extend hospitality to such a person?

In what ways does the love of Christ challenge you to love those you may have regarded as unlovable?

A
Application for Today

More than two decades ago, four Christians traveled together to various nations, including Israel. Their travel plans took them first to Spain for several days. Their flight from Barcelona to Tel Aviv included a plane change in Cairo. To their surprise, as they boarded the plane in Barcelona and settled into their business-class seats, they noticed every other person on the flight seemed to be Muslim, dressed in traditional Arab garb.

One of the Christians asked a flight attendant about this and learned the entire plane, except for their few seats, had been booked as far as Cairo by Muslims on their way ultimately to Mecca for the hajj—an annual Muslim ritual that represented a lifelong pilgrimage for most of those on board. At the time of normal Muslim prayers, as many of the Muslim men as possible got out of their seats and knelt in the aisles of the plane, while prayers were voiced by a Muslim cleric at the front of the business-class section.

The Christians remained in their seats, suddenly aware of how much they stood out as aliens to their fellow passengers.

They discussed their feelings after they landed in Cairo, and admitted to one another they felt just as much distrust and prejudice *toward* the Muslim passengers as they had felt *from* the Muslims. Two of the Christians admitted feeling some fear. One felt trapped. Another said she had felt anger—as if she had been violated in some way.

"I'm glad the Lord didn't ask me to witness to the passengers next to me about Christ," one of the Christians said.

"I'm not sure I would have heard Him if He had told me," another admitted.

Can you imagine yourself being in such a situation?

How would you have felt?

What would have been your response if the Lord had said, "Give the gospel to the person across the aisle from you"?

S
Supplementary Scriptures to Consider

To know God is leading you to go beyond the cultural norm is one thing. To convince others God is leading you is sometimes an entirely different issue, as Peter discovered:

Now the apostles and brethren who were in Judea heard
that the Gentiles had also received the word of God. And
when Peter came up to Jerusalem, those of the circumcision
contended with him, saying, "You went in to uncircumcised
men and ate with them!"

But Peter explained it to them in order from the beginning. . . .

When they heard these things they became silent; and they
glorified God, saying, "Then God has also granted to the
Gentiles repentance to life" (Acts 11:1–4,18).

• Have you ever been criticized for taking the gospel into an area where
  others thought you should not go? (Be specific.) What happened as the
  result of your efforts? How did you respond to the criticism you received?

• Have you ever been criticized for reaching out to a person whom others
  perceived to be dangerous or inappropriate for you to befriend for the
  sake of the gospel? (Be specific.) What happened as a result of your
  witness? How did you respond to the criticism you received?

The pattern of ministry for Paul was to go first with the gospel message to synagogues and teach the Jews about Jesus' sacrificial atoning death and resurrection. When Jews rejected the message, he did what was unthinkable to his Jewish brethren—he turned to the Gentiles in that city:

> Then Paul and Barnabas grew bold and said, "It was
> necessary that the word of God should be spoken to you first;
> but since you reject it, and judge yourselves unworthy of
> everlasting life, behold, we turn to the Gentiles. For so the
> Lord has commanded us:
>> 'I have set you as a light to the Gentiles,
>> That you should be for salvation to the ends of the earth.'"
> Now when the Gentiles heard this, they were glad and
> glorified the word of the Lord. And as many as had been
> appointed to eternal life believed (Acts 13:46–48).

• Paul said it was necessary *that the word of God should be spoken to you first* (Acts 13:46). How do you feel about that statement? Have you ever felt the leading of the Lord to go to a particular person or group of people first with your gospel message before going to another person or group? What was the result?

• For what purposes might God call a person to share the gospel with people who are of *like* culture, background, language, or intellect? For what purposes might God call a person to share the gospel with those who are from a very *different* culture, background, or level of education?

- Is it possible to influence someone who is *supposed* to be a light, but who doesn't *want* to shine as a light?

Paul had every intention of going east to preach in Asia, but the Holy Spirit led him in the opposite direction:

> Now when they had gone through Phrygia and the region of Galatia, they were forbidden by the Holy Spirit to preach the word in Asia. After they had come to Mysia, they tried to go into Bithynia, but the Spirit did not permit them. So passing by Mysia, they came down to Troas. And a vision appeared to Paul in the night. A man of Macedonia stood and pleaded with him, saying, "Come over to Macedonia and help us." Now after he had seen the vision, immediately we sought to go to Macedonia, concluding that the Lord had called us to preach the gospel to them" (Acts 16:6–10).

- Paul was not a man who operated on whim or notion. He had a reputation for being a reasonable, highly educated intellectual. He no doubt had reasoned that after making a successful missionary journey to the west of Antioch, it was time to take the gospel eastward to Asia. God had a different plan. Have you ever reasoned one way only to have the Holy Spirit take you in an entirely different direction? What were the results?

• The Holy Spirit led Paul and his fellow missionaries step by step. The Spirit closed the door to Asia but they were allowed to head toward Mysia. The Spirit closed the door to Bithynia and caused them to pass by Mysia. In Troas, the Holy Spirit gave Paul a vision and call to Macedonia. Have you ever experienced a step-by-step leading of the Lord? What happened? As you look back on that experience, can you see a reason for what God did?

I
Introspection and Implications

1. How do you determine to whom you are going to share the gospel of Jesus Christ? What criteria do you use? How do you discern whether you are being led of the Holy Spirit or led by your own human desires?

2. In what ways is it difficult to overcome your own prejudices?

3. In what ways is it difficult to hear and heed the Holy Spirit when His directives seem to counteract your own reasoning ability or intellect?

4. Have you ever prayed the Lord would *not* call you to a particular place or to share the gospel with a particular person? What happened?

5. How do you stay pure as a person and still reach out to impure people? How does the church stay pure and still invite sinners into its midst?

6. How do you experience the Holy Spirit saying "no" to you or to your plans?

C
Communicating the Good News

How important is it to not become discouraged when those with whom you share the gospel reject what you say and likely reject you personally? Jesus said this in sending out His disciples with news of the kingdom: "Whoever will not receive you nor hear your words, when you depart from that house or city, shake off the dust from your feet" (Matthew 10:14). What does Jesus' statement mean to you?

How do you determine who you will support as a missionary?

How do you and others in your church determine where, when, and to whom you will reach out in your evangelistic efforts?

Lesson #6

EMPOWERED TO OVERCOME DEATH

Emulation: successfully duplicating or imitating what you have seen someone else do

B
Bible Focus

> At Joppa there was a certain disciple named Tabitha, which
> is translated Dorcas. This woman was full of good works and
> charitable deeds which she did. But it happened in those days
> that she became sick and died. When they had washed her,
> they laid her in an upper room. And since Lydda was near
> Joppa, and the disciples had heard that Peter was there, they
> sent two men to him, imploring him not to delay in coming to
> them. Then Peter arose and went with them. When he had
> come, they brought him to the upper room. And all the widows
> stood by him weeping, showing the tunics and garments which
> Dorcas had made while she was with them. But Peter put them
> all out, and knelt down and prayed. And turning to the body
> he said, "Tabitha, arise." And she opened her eyes, and when
> she saw Peter she sat up. Then he gave her his hand and lifted
> her up; and when he had called the saints and widows, he
> presented her alive. And it became known throughout all
> Joppa, and many believed on the Lord. So it was that he
> stayed many days in Joppa with Simon, a tanner (Acts
> 9:36–43).

One of the traditions associated with baptism at the time of Jesus was the
giving of a new tunic to those who were baptized. The repentant shed their
old garment as they entered the waters of renewal and commitment, and
upon emerging from the waters, they were given a *new garment* symbolic of
their changed life.

The apostle Paul later referred to this traditional custom in writing to the
Ephesians. "As the truth is in Jesus: that you put off, concerning your former
conduct, the old man which grows corrupt according to the deceitful lusts, and
be renewed in the spirit of your mind, and that you put on the new man which
was created according to God, in true righteousness and holiness" (Ephesians
4:21–24).

It was likely this type of baptism-related garment that Dorcas lovingly and
generously made by hand. She undoubtedly was a faithful and talented woman
who used her skill in sewing to serve the Lord. Garments in the Middle East
are often embellished with embroidery, and the garments Dorcas made may
also have been beautifully embroidered, truly making them original works of
art.

When Dorcas died, and Jesus' disciples heard Peter was in the area, they
sent for him and he came immediately. The scene was no doubt reminiscent of

an experience in Peter's close association with Jesus. Peter had been with Jesus at the time the twelve-year-old daughter of a synagogue leader named Jairus died. Jesus had gone to Jairus' house to find people gathered in mourning and weeping. Jesus had put everyone out of the room except Jairus and his wife, Peter, James, and John. Then Jesus had taken the child by the hand and said to her, "*Talitha, cumi*," which is translated, "Little girl, I say to you, arise." (See Mark 5:36–43.)

When Peter arrived at Lydda, he found mourning and great weeping. He put all those present out of the room, and then Peter used Dorcas' Aramaic name Tabitha and said, "Tabitha, cumi," translated "Tabitha, arise." She opened her eyes, sat up, and when Peter gave her his hand, she stood up and Peter presented her alive to the saints and widows gathered outside.

Peter did what he had seen Jesus do. He said what he had heard Jesus say. He believed as Jesus had believed. And he experienced the same results as when Jesus had raised Jairus' daughter from her deathbed.

What have you seen Jesus do?

What have you heard Jesus speak to your heart with His Spirit and through God's Word?

What do you believe can happen when you do what Jesus did and say what Jesus said, believing in Him with your whole heart?

A
Application for Today

"Copycat! Copycat!"

It was a taunt we didn't want to hear as a child; generally, a critical appraisal by our peers that we couldn't think on our own.

As the years passed, however, and we learned imitation is one of the finest forms of flattery, we wanted others to copy our style and mannerisms. We copied others as well. That's the way we fit in with our peers. As adults and parents, we traded in the phrase *copy cat* for *role model*, and especially in dealing with our children, we now earnestly seek to be copied.

Jesus said to His disciples, "Do you not believe that I am in the Father, and the Father in Me? The words that I speak to you I do not speak on My own authority; but the Father who dwells in Me does the works" (John 14:10). Jesus went on to say to His disciples, "Most assuredly, I say to you, whatever you ask the Father in My name He will give you. Until now you have asked nothing in My name. Ask, and you will receive, that your joy may be full" (John 16:23–24). Jesus invites us to be a *copy cat* of His words and deeds, to follow his example as a model for our lives. He invites us to make His identity our own. As we are transformed into His likeness, our joy will be *full*!

Is it good or bad to copy someone?

How do you determine whom to copy for good results?
Whom do you copy today in your behavior, beliefs, and style?
Who is copying you?

S
Supplementary Scriptures to Consider

As Paul was being transported to Rome for a trial, his ship encountered an intense storm. After two weeks of being tossed about on the Adriatic Sea, Paul spoke to those on board:

> As day was about to dawn, Paul implored them all to take food, saying, "Today is the fourteenth day you have waited and continued without food, and eaten nothing. Therefore I urge you to take nourishment, for this is for your survival, since not a hair will fall from the head of any of you."

> When it was day, they did not recognize the land; but they observed a bay with a beach, onto which they planned to run the ship if possible.

> And the soldiers' plan was to kill the prisoners, lest any of them should swim away and escape. But the centurion, wanting to save Paul, kept them from their purpose, and commanded that those who could swim should jump overboard first and get to land, and the rest, some on boards and some on parts of the ship. And so it was that they all escaped safely to land" (Acts 27:33–34, 39, 42–44).

• Have you ever had someone intervene on your behalf to keep you from experiencing physical or emotional harm at the hands of another person? In what ways can you see in retrospect God was using that person for His purposes?

• The Holy Spirit gave Paul a survival plan. (Read the entire story of Paul's perilous journey and shipwreck in Acts 27.) Have you ever experienced the Holy Spirit giving you a plan for how best to survive a natural catastrophe, a major crisis, or a difficult period? (Cite a specific example.) What happened?

• Have you ever survived a harrowing experience in which you very easily could have died? What happened? How did your surviving confirm to you God had helped you? Did you feel confirmation that God still had a purpose for your life?

Almost immediately after Paul survived shipwreck, he was faced with a different problem that people around him considered to be life-threatening:

> Now when they had escaped, they then found out that the
> island was called Malta. And the natives showed us unusual
> kindness; for they kindled a fire and made us all welcome,
> because of the rain that was falling and because of the cold.
> But when Paul had gathered a bundle of sticks and laid them
> on the fire, a viper came out because of the heat, and fastened
> on his hand. So when the natives saw the creature hanging
> from his hand, they said to one another, "No doubt this man is
> a murderer, whom, though he has escaped the sea, yet justice

does not allow to live." But he shook off the creature into the fire and suffered no harm. However, they were expecting that he would swell up or suddenly fall down dead. But after they had looked for a long time and saw no harm come to him, they changed their minds and said that he was a god (Acts 28:1–6).

• Have you ever had people draw a conclusion that you deserved to have something bad happen to you? How did you respond? What does God's Word say about such a conclusion made about a Christian?

• Human opinion is fickle! One minute the citizens of Malta were concluding Paul was an evil murderer deserving to die and the next minute they were calling him a god. Have you ever been on the roller coaster of human opinion about who you are? How did you respond? How can negative human opinion kill a person's reputation or effectiveness? How can undue positive human praise kill a person's humility or reliance on the Lord? How important is it to be concerned only with God's opinion, not human opinion, in matters related to your own purpose and effectiveness?

• Have you ever had a close encounter that could have killed you? What happened? Why do you believe you are alive and not dead?

I
Introspection and Implications

1. Most of the time we think of death as being physical. What other aspects of our lives are subject to death? (For example: Can relationships die? Can jobs or careers die? Can a reputation be killed? Can a worthy goal be snuffed out?)

2. We human beings sometimes conclude that a person *died before their time*. Does God draw such a conclusion?

3. Why should we do our utmost to fight against death wherever and whenever we encounter it? How does your view of eternity impact your feelings toward death?

4. If you had been present when Dorcas died, would you have sent for Peter? Why or why not?

5. How do you respond to the phrase *life-threatening illness*?

6. A woman once said: "There's only a fraction of a moment when a person with a serious disease goes from getting worse to getting better." Reflect on that statement. What do you believe causes the turnaround? Consider the statement: "There's only a faction of a moment when a person who feels emotionally as if he has been dying suddenly feels that he has started living again." What causes the turnaround?

C
Communicating the Good News

How important is the message of *eternal life* to your personal proclamation of the gospel? How important should it be?

How important is the message of *abundant life* (See John 10:10) to your personal proclamation of the gospel? How important should it be?

How do the phrases *abundant life* and *eternal life* complement each other?

LESSON #7

EMPOWERED TO ENDURE AND PERSEVERE

*Endurance: the ability to bear prolonged
exertion, pain, hardship, or suffering
Perseverance: the ability to continue
believing and doing what you know to be
right, regardless of difficulties or setbacks*

B
Bible Focus

> And they brought them to the magistrates, and said,
> "These men, being Jews, exceedingly trouble our city; and
> they teach customs which are not lawful for us, being
> Romans, to receive or observe." Then the multitude rose up
> together against them; and the magistrates tore off their
> clothes and commanded them to be beaten with rods. And
> when they had laid many stripes on them, they threw them
> into prison, commanding the jailer to keep them securely.
> Having received such a charge, he put them into the inner
> prison and fastened their feet in the stocks.
>
> But at midnight Paul and Silas were praying and singing
> hymns to God, and the prisoners were listening to them.
> Suddenly there was a great earthquake, so that the founda-
> tions of the prison were shaken; and immediately all the
> doors were opened and everyone's chains were loosed. And
> the keeper of the prison, awaking from sleep and seeing the
> prison doors open, supposing the prisoners had fled, drew
> his sword and was about to kill himself.
>
> But Paul called with a loud voice, saying, "Do yourself
> no harm, for we are all here."
>
> Then he called for a light, ran in, and fell down trembling
> before Paul and Silas. And he brought them out and said,
> "Sirs, what must I do to be saved?"
>
> So they said, "Believe on the Lord Jesus Christ, and you
> will be saved, you and your household." Then they spoke the
> word of the Lord to him and to all who were in his house.
> And he took them the same hour of the night and washed
> their stripes. And immediately he and all his family were
> baptized. Now when he had brought them into his house, he
> set food before them; and he rejoiced, having believed in
> God with all his household (Acts 16:20–34).

One of the most dramatic series of miracles in all the New Testament
took place in a matter of hours in the Greek city of Philippi. The apostle
Paul had cast out a spirit of divination from a slave girl, and her owner
had dragged Paul and his traveling companion Silas to the authorities in
anger that he had been stripped of his ability to make money from the
girl's divination power. Based solely on the slave owner's accusations

and his ability to incite a mob, the magistrates had ordered Paul and Silas to be beaten with rods and thrown into an *inner prison*, likely what we would call a dungeon, where their feet were *fastened* in stocks—a procedure that not only kept the prisoner secure but inflicted further pain (Acts 16:24).

Knowing the physical pain inflicted upon Paul and Silas, it was amazing that they were not only alive after receiving *many stripes*, but also, they had the strength to pray and sing hymns, obviously with a purpose of sharing the gospel with other prisoners who were *listening to them* (Acts 16:23, 25)!

At midnight, *a great earthquake* shook the foundations of the prison, causing all of the doors to spring open and the chains of the stocks to be loosed (Acts 16:26).

The prison was shaken by a powerful earthquake, and it was astounding that the walls didn't cave in and Paul and Silas and the other prisoners were still alive!

The keeper of the prison, who was responsible for securing his prisoners or face death himself, feared all his prisoners had escaped. He was about to kill himself when Paul cried out, *"We are all here"* (Acts 16:28).

Surprisingly, no one had tried to escape!

The prison keeper was astonished. No doubt he had heard the prayers and singing of Paul and Silas. He knew what they believed, and he asked, *"Sirs, what must I do to be saved?"* (Acts 16:30). Paul and Silas took the opportunity to speak the word of the Lord directly to him and all in his house. In that same hour, the prison keeper washed the wounds of Paul and Silas, and in turn, they led the prison keeper and his family into the waters of baptism. They ate together and rejoiced, likely until dawn.

God used the miracle to quickly and completely change hearts.

Paul and Silas had endured tremendous injustice and physical torture. Yet, they reaped a harvest of souls and joy.

What are the keys to enduring hardship and to persevering in your faith through difficult times?

Key number one: *Prayer*. Voice your petitions to God, with faith.

Key number two: *Praise*. Give expression to your faith in God in words and in songs.

Key number three: *Purpose*. Have as your core purpose in life the sharing of God's Word and the message of salvation.

These are the keys that activate God's miracle-working power to open doors and bring about opportunities for the gospel to advance. These are the keys that lead to solace in suffering and the healing of wounds. These are the keys that result in great rejoicing, on earth and in heaven.

A
Application for Today

A man once found himself in a city jail, falsely accused and unjustly arrested. He was the only prisoner in the jail that night. One jailer was on duty in the office nearby. The man didn't know what else to do but pray. As part of his prayer, he reminded the Lord of Paul and Silas. He then sang every praise chorus he knew, put his head down on his rolled-up jacket, and went to sleep. About a half hour later, he heard the clanging of his jail cell door. He looked up to see the door to his cell open and the jailer motioning for him to exit. "You're free to go," the jailer said.

"Really?" the man replied as he stood up and prepared to walk out of the cell. "What happened?"

"Well," the jailer replied, "it seems the person who called the police and accused you had a change of heart, went to the judge's house about an hour ago, and rang his doorbell repeatedly until the judge got up. He told the judge an error had been made, and the judge called us and said to let you go."

"Really?" the man repeated, wondering if he was in a dream.

"I argued with him," the jailer said. "I told the judge I didn't know what to do with the forms in triplicate I had already filled out on you. He told me that wasn't his problem and to release you immediately."

The man suddenly realized he was awake and he turned and said abruptly to the jailer, "Do you know Jesus as your Savior?" The jailer grinned. "Yeah, I do. I heard you praying and singing in there and I know the Bible story, and frankly, I'm not surprised things turned out like this. I'm just glad we didn't have to go through an earthquake."

"Well, if you're not supposed to get saved tonight, what was this all about?" the man mused aloud.

"Maybe so we'll both be able to tell our grandkids someday we know what happened to Paul and Silas can happen to a person in *our* time."

There are times when God delivers us from ever having to suffer. His message is one of divine protection.

There are other times when God allows us to experience a degree of suffering and delivers us from the full agony of it. His message is one of mercy.

There are still other times when God allows us to go through intense suffering so we might witness to others that, even in the midst of great pain, we believe in God and trust in His saving power. His message is one of grace.

Are you going through a difficult time?

How are you handling it?

What message of God are you conveying to others around you?

S
Supplementary Scriptures to Consider

Jesus taught His disciples:

> "Behold, I send you out as sheep in the midst of wolves. Therefore be wise as serpents and harmless as doves. But beware of men, for they will deliver you up to councils and scourge you in their synagogues. You will be brought before governors and kings for My sake, as a testimony to them and to the Gentiles.

> "Now brother will deliver up brother to death, and a father his child; and children will rise up against parents and cause them to be put to death. And you will be hated by all for My name's sake. But he who endures to the end will be saved. When they persecute you in this city, flee to another. For assuredly, I say to you, you will not have gone through the cities of Israel before the Son of Man comes" (Matthew 10:16–18,21–23).

• What does it mean to you to *endure to the end* (Matthew 10:22)?

• Even as Jesus taught His disciples to *endure to the end* and be *saved*, he advised them to *flee to another* city when they are persecuted (Matthew 10:22–23). How do you resolve what appear to be conflicting messages? Is it possible to endure in faith *and* flee in the flesh simultaneously?

- How do you determine when to take a stand and when to walk away from an argument or conflict? How did Paul and Silas both make a stand and walk away? (Read the rest of the story in Acts 16.)

- What does it mean to you to be *wise as serpents and harmless as doves* (Matthew 10:16)?

- In what specific ways must we rely on the Holy Spirit to guide us in our decisions related to persevering and enduring?

How important it is for us to persevere in our prayers for others! Prayer and miracles go hand in hand:

> Now about that time Herod the king stretched out his hand to harass some from the church. Then he killed James the brother of John with the sword. And because he saw that it pleased the Jews, he proceeded further to seize Peter also. Now it was during the Days of Unleavened Bread. So when he had arrested him, he put him in prison, and delivered him to four squads of solders to keep him, intending to bring him before the people after Passover.
>
> Peter was therefore kept in prison, but constant prayer was offered to God for him by the church. And when Herod was about to bring him out, that night Peter was sleeping, bound with two chains between two soldiers; and the guards before the door were keeping the prison. Now behold, an angel of the Lord stood by him, and a light shone in the prison; and he struck Peter on the side and raised him up, saying, "Arise, quickly!" And his chains fell off his hands. Then the angel said to him, "Gird yourself and tie on your sandals"; and so he did. And he said to him, "Put on your garment and follow me." So he went out and followed him, and did not know that what was done by the angel was real, but thought he was seeing a vision. When they were past the first and the second guard posts, they came to the iron gate that leads to the city, which opened to them of its own accord; and they went out and went down one street, and immediately the angel departed from him.
>
> And when Peter had come to himself, he said, "Now I know for certain that the Lord has sent His angel, and has delivered me from the hand of Herod and from all the expectation of the Jewish people."
>
> So, when he had considered this, he came to the house of Mary, the mother of John whose surname was Mark, where many were gathered together praying.
>
> And he said, "Go, tell these things to James and to the brethren." And he departed and went to another place.
>
> Then, as soon as it was day, there was no small stir among the soldiers about what had become of Peter. But when Herod had searched for him and not found him, he examined the guards and commanded that they should be put to death. And

he went down from Judea to Caesarea, and stayed there (Acts 12:1–12,17–19).

• How important is prayer to our ability to endure tough times? How important is prayer to our ability to persevere in what we know to be true about Jesus Christ?

• Has the Lord led you to intercede in prayer for Christians in other nations who are undergoing persecution? How are you praying? Are you steadfast in your prayers? What are you trusting God to do?

• Has anyone ever interceded in prayer for you to endure a difficult experi-ence? What happened?

I
Introspection and Implications

1. How difficult is it to endure physical suffering? In what ways do you rely on the Holy Spirit to help you when you are in pain or are facing illness?

2. How difficult is it to endure open criticism or unwarranted accusations from other people? In what ways do you rely on the Holy Spirit to show you how—*and when*—to respond?

3. What do you do when you emerge on the other side of suffering or crisis? In the case of Paul and Silas, the magistrates sent word the morning after the earthquake that the prison keeper was to let them go. Paul said, "They have beaten us openly, uncondemned Romans, and have thrown us into prison. And now do they put us out secretly? No indeed! Let them come themselves and get us out" (Acts 16:37). The magistrates came to plead with Paul personally. Would you have taken this tactic? Is it important when you are falsely humiliated or criticized in a very public way to seek an equally public apology? Why or why not?

4. Have you ever been tempted to give up something you knew Jesus had led you to do or establish? What did you do? How did you make your decision? What happened?

5. To what extent does God ask us to endure consequences that are related to problems of our own making? Where does human stubbornness end and faithful perseverance begin?

C
Communicating the Good News

There's an old phrase, "I never promised you a rose garden." Along with roses come thorns. Along with sunshine comes rain. How important is it as we share the gospel of Jesus Christ to be realistic with people about problems that may still arise in their lives after their conversion experience?

In what ways are we to strengthen people in their faith so they will be able to withstand persecution, conflict, and tough times?

In what ways—and to what extent—does the Holy Spirit challenge us to help other believers endure the problems they encounter and to persevere in their relationship with Christ Jesus?

Notes to Leaders
of Small Groups

As the leader of a small discussion group, think of yourself as a facilitator with three main roles:

- Get the discussion started

- Involve every person in the group

- Encourage an open, candid discussion that remains focused on the Bible

You certainly don't need to be the person with all the answers! In truth, much of your role is to ask questions, such as:

- What impacted you most in this lesson?

- What part of the lesson did you find troubling?

- What part of the lesson was encouraging or insightful?

- What part of the lesson would you like to explore further?

Express to the group at the outset of your study that your goal as a group is to gain new insights into God's Word—this is not the forum for defending a point of doctrine or a theological opinion. Stay focused on what God's Word says and means. The purpose of the study is also to share insights of how to apply God's Word to everyday life. *Every* person in the group can and should contribute—the collective wisdom that flows from Bible-focused discussion is often very rich and deep.

Seek to create an environment in which every member of the group feels free to ask questions of other members to gain greater understanding. Encourage group members to voice their appreciation to one another for new insights gained, and to be supportive of one another personally. Take the lead in doing this. Genuinely appreciate and value the contributions each person makes.

You may want to begin each study by having one or more members of the group read through the section provided under "Bible Focus." Ask the group specifically if it desires to discuss any of the questions under the "Application for Today" section, the "Supplemental Scriptures to Consider" section, the "Introspection and Implications" and "Communicating the Good News" section. You do not need to come to a definitive conclusion or consensus about any question asked in this study. Rather, encourage your group if it does not have a satisfactory Bible-based answer to a question that the group engage in further asking, seeking, and knocking strategies to discover the answers. Remember the words of Jesus: "Ask, and it will be given to you; seek, and you will find; knock, and it will be opened to you. For everyone who asks receives, and he who seeks finds, and to him who knocks it will be opened" (Matthew 7:7–8).

Finally, open and close your study with prayer. Ask the Holy Spirit, whom Jesus called the Spirit of Truth, to guide your discussion and to reveal what is of eternal benefit to you individually and as a group. As you close your time together, ask the Holy Spirit to seal to your remembrance what you have read and studied, and to show you ways in the upcoming days, weeks, and months to apply what you have studied to your daily life and relationships.

General Themes for the Lessons

Each lesson in this study has one or more core themes. Continually pull the group back to these themes. You can do this by asking simple questions, such as, "How does that relate to_____?", "How does that help us better understand the concept of _____?", or "In what ways does that help us apply the principle of _____?"

A summary of general themes or concepts in each lesson follows:

Lesson #1
EMPOWERED TO WITNESS

Personal witness

Empowerment by the Holy Spirit

Experiencing guidance from the Holy Spirit about to whom and in what ways we are to give witness to Christ Jesus

Lesson #2

EMPOWERED TO SERVE

The nature of Christ-centered service to others

Service to believers versus service to unbelievers

The nature of a servant's heart

The role of loving service in building up the church and expanding the kingdom

Lesson #3

EMPOWERED TO HEAL

The multi-faceted nature of illness

The multi-faceted nature of health

Using our gifts—both natural and spiritual—as agents of healing

The role of faith in the healing process

Lesson #4

EMPOWERED TO DELIVER FROM EVIL

Identifying, confronting, and overcoming evil

What it means to truly be delivered from evil

Discerning the future

Genuine godly prophecy versus occult divination

Lesson #5

EMPOWERED TO HURDLE MAN-MADE BARRIERS

Overcoming prejudice

Man-made barriers versus God's commandments regarding relationships to avoid

Personal barriers we construct to avoid sharing the gospel

Lesson #6

EMPOWERED TO OVERCOME DEATH

The many types of death

The power of faith, hope, and love to promote life

What it means to speak faith in a life-threatening situation

Lesson #7

EMPOWERED TO ENDURE AND PERSEVERE

Endurance through tough times

Perseverance in faith

Interceding in prayer with steadfast commitment

The role of praise in endurance and perseverance

NOTES